Can you Spot the Leopard?

African Masks

Prestel · Munich · New York

In Africa there are many peoples who have mask ceremonies for different occasions. These can be **joyful**, like a harvest festival, or **sad**, like a funeral, or **serious**, when the land is threatened by drought, or even **dangerous**, when the people are trying to ward off witches. Masks are also important in young people's lives when they come of age and are accepted into the adult world.

Some mask ceremonies are to help people through difficult times. Some teach people about the past and where human beings first came from. Some are about the meaning of life and death and some warn of what will happen if people do not behave as they should. Above all, masks are used in ceremonies where the wisdom and experience of the older generation is being passed down to the younger generation. For those taking part, masks can represent many things: their ancestors, good and evil spirits, dangerous witches and wizards, goblins, bush and water spirits or even illnesses.

African masks can have **human** faces, **animal** faces or be a mixture of the two put together. Sometimes it is not very easy to spot which animal is meant. For example, the mask in the bottom right hand corner of page 16 has a human face, crocodile teeth, buffalo ears, antelope horns and the rolled-up tail of a chameleon. Masks are almost always carved from one piece of wood and cover the wearer's face or the whole head. They can be painted in just one colour or in many different colours; sometimes they are also decorated with cowry shells or glass beads. The mask is then finished off with plant fibres or pieces of material that completely hide the wearer. Mask ceremonies are always accompanied by music, singing and dancing. This is why we talk of mask dances and mask dancers. Usually there will be several masks in a ceremony either performing one at a time or all at once in a large procession.

Why do so many masks represent animals? Because the ancestors, the bush spirits and the water spirits like best to appear as animals. And whatever form of animal they take, that is how they then seem to be: as swift as an antelope or as silent as a leopard, as wise as an **elephant** or as greedy as a **hyena**, able to live in both water and on dry land just like a crocodile. The moment a dancer puts on a mask he stops being himself. As long as the dance lasts, the dancer behaves like the animal his mask represents. It is as though he himself becomes a **crocodile** or a **snake** and this shows in the way he dances: the sawfish twirls rapidly around while the elephant rages to and fro.

But not everyone is allowed to wear a mask or to carve a mask or even to touch one and usually not everyone in a village is even allowed to watch a mask ceremony. Masks are seen as sacred — many of them as extremely dangerous, too. So masks are almost always kept and looked after by secret societies who store them in special places and it is the members of those secret societies who then perform the mask dances.

Only certain people may be members of a secret society and these people must never say a word about what they do. Outsiders are not allowed to know anything about the society. In Africa members are usually men, and they are prepared for membership when they are still boys. But it would be wrong to imagine that this is how it has always been! For, in fact, we know from many African tales that long ago it was the women who were in charge of the masks and who were looked up to for their wisdom: they were the ones who knew how to till the soil, sow the seeds and harvest the crops. But then the men became envious of the women, and, fearing that they were losing their influence in their own community, they set up secret societies. And that is why — with few exceptions — ever since then women and girls take no part in mask ceremonies.

Patiently standing one on top of the other, it looks as though these animals
are all helping the littlest one to see far into the distance.

Right at the very bottom there is a helmet in the shape of a person's head with eyes,
nose and an open mouth. The person wearing the mask looks out through the mouth.

The mask seems to be made out of alternating light and dark wood but in fact,
like most African masks, it is made out of just one piece of wood.

Before he starts carving the wood, the artist must already know what the finished
mask is going to look like. Where should one animal's legs end and where should
the next one's head start?

African carvers are extraordinarily skilled in working with wood.
Can you see which animals the artist has painted and which ones not?

The Yoruba wear these masks for their *epa* festival. This is held in March every
second year to honour their great warriors and to increase the fertility and
well-being of the people.

At some point during the festival the mask dancers usually have to jump down
from a wall of earth. But they have to be extremely careful to keep their balance.
The Yoruba believe that if the dancer falls over it is a sign that bad luck is on its way.

The mask dancer has to be a real acrobat, because as well as the mask he has a costume
of plant fibres and cloth covering his entire body. Some of these masks can weigh
over 25 kilos, so the dancer also has to be very strong. If he were weak and clumsy
he would soon just trip over himself.

Just look at all the animals on the mask !

Who do you think is in charge ?

Which animals can you see here?

You'll find them almost all again in other places in this book.

A proper family

A long time ago, according to Bamana legend, a creature called Tyiwara lived on this earth. It was half human being, half antelope and taught the people how to till the fields. For some years everything went well and the harvest was plentiful. But then the people began to neglect their fields and to waste the food. Tyiwara was so sad about this that it hid away under the ground. Then the people were sorry for the way they had behaved. In order to please Tyiwara and to thank it for all the good things it had done, the Bamana carved small antelopes and fixed them on to woven head-dresses.

Every year when the crops are being sown and harvested the Bamana hold mask ceremonies in the fields. Two young dancers wear carved antelope masks on their heads, one male, one female. The dancers' faces and bodies are completely hidden under costumes made of plant tendrils, representing the rain that is so rare in their country. A farmer must have stamina and be patient, strong and far-sighted. In order to find the best farmer in the village, the Bamana hold a competition: Tyiwara encourages the competitors and the farmer who finishes working his part of the field first is the winner.

Of course real antelopes don't have such short legs, but the artist who carved these head-dresses wanted to emphasise their heads and necks. The father antelope looks as though he is just about to leap up: his powerful neck is tense and bent back, his horns point proudly upwards and his mane flutters wildly in the wind. The mother antelope, on the other hand, is quite calm — carrying her young on her back.

Is it a **male** or a **female** kid?

Just look at those teeth!

The leopard mask looking at us on the right seems so fierce and ferocious. We can almost feel how worked up it is, ready to pounce on its prey. It is enough to give anyone goose pimples! Its light and dark spots look just like the patterned fur of a real leopard. The face is dominated by its large, square mouth with lips drawn right back to show us its huge, threatening teeth. These were probably originally painted in black and white, but the white paint has worn away by now. Across Africa the leopard is seen as intelligent and brave but, above all, as dangerous, for it can also kill people. It is an outstandingly skilled hunter and can stalk to within a few

metres of its prey without being noticed before it suddenly attacks. So kings, leaders and others responsible for law and order have often chosen the leopard as a sign of their power. This mask was made by the Dogon, who live in Mali in West Africa, while the leopard mask up above this block of text is from Zaire. It looks very different, consisting of a cap and a robe, both made from bast decorated with dots and some lines. Bast is the name for the fibrous under-surface of the bark of a tree, which is separated from the bark and then beaten and flattened. Which do you think would be easier: to make a mask like this or to carve one out of wood?

Cocks **crow** in Africa too to greet the

When a family member has died, the Mossi in Burkina Faso perform special mask ceremonies with cockerel masks which, for them, embody the spirits of their ancestors. Like many other peoples, the Mossi believe that a person's body dies, but not his spirit. They believe the spirit lives on in a different, invisible world and that it can still take part in the lives of those left behind, doing good deeds — but not only good deeds — for if the family forgets their ancestors, the spirits will punish them by spoiling the harvest or sending illness. So a family must always be respectful and humble in their thoughts about their ancestors and pray for their blessing. And, in other ways too, the family left behind must behave well and never harm others, for the ancestral spirits would immediately see they were punished if they did.

Hasn't the artist made a wonderful cockerel's head?

The colours and the patterns almost make it look alive. If it could it would just open its beak and crow — but its beak is tied at the end. Why? Unfortunately we don't know. But, whatever the case, its comb is swelling magnificently: boldly curved and encrusted in thick, reddish-brown pigment.

sun

each morning.

SSsome SSSSSSnakes are soooooooo long ...

Pythons are the longest snakes in Africa and can grow to over five metres. The snake masks of the Bwa in Burkina Faso are nearly as long. It is just about impossible to get the whole of it into one picture. And even these are carved out of one piece of wood!

The story goes that once a man, trying to escape enemy warriors who were attacking his village, took refuge underground in a snake's lair. The snake protected him and fed him for two weeks. When the man returned to his village the soothsayer told him that as a sign of gratitude he should make a mask in the form of that snake and perform a dance in its honour.

These snake masks are worn by young men who already start practising for this when they are children. To stop the snake from toppling over, the dancers hold a string between their teeth which is attached to the mask at both ends. The Bwa use these snake masks for many different occasions and on market days mask dances are performed to entertain the villagers and the visiting traders. Sometimes there are as many as 15 masks altogether! The snake's head on the right has been made with love and attention: first the artist carved circles, triangles, lines and zig-zags into the wood and then picked them out in red, black and white.

Who's that dancing on my head?

The little monkey better watch out or he'll fall right off! And it looks as though he knows it too. Look at the way he is baring his teeth — scared? — just showing off? It's not very easy to say what kind of an animal the little pest is dancing around on. It could be a leopard or a hyena. Whatever the case, it looks rather out of breath, as though it is gasping for air. And the little monkey seems to be pulling so hard on its ears that its eyes are bulging.

In Zaire, when Yaka boys come of age, there is a whole series of ceremonies accompanied by mask dances. And the very last mask to appear — delighting and surprising the villagers — is the most beautiful of all, called the Mbala mask. The two animals on this mask really seem like circus acrobats. The cleverly painted decorations on the monkey look like a costume. The little rascal has wooden arms, legs and head: the rest of him is made out of soft bast. The two animals were first made separately and then joined together. Behind the mask's mouth there is a wooden handle that the dancer uses to hold the mask in front of his face during the performance.

A fairy-tale from West Africa

Once upon a time there was a **huntsman** who went far into the bush. After a while he came to a deep ditch: caught in it there was a **leopard**, an **antelope**, a snake and a man. "Huntsman, help me out of here," cried the leopard. "If you do I'll always be good to you." So the huntsman lifted him out. Then the antelope cried: "I will also reward you if you help me." So the huntsman lifted her out and then the snake as well, who also said she would show him her gratitude. Now only the man was left in the ditch and the huntsman thought to himself: "If I have already rescued three animals then I can't let a human being die, especially not when he looks just like me." So he helped the man as well. To show how grateful he was, the leopard soon brought the huntsman two beautiful gazelles, that he had caught for him. And the antelope he had saved also kept her promise: buried in a place where she sometimes ate a little earth, as all antelopes do, she had once found a pot of gold which belonged to God's brother, Anangama. Now she fetched this and gave it to the huntsman.

But the man that the huntsman had rescued saw this and went to Anangama and said: "The antelope has dug up your pot of gold and has given it to a huntsman." Angrily Anangama sent out word for the huntsman to be captured and tied up. So that is what happened.

But that night the snake came quietly to the huntsman, bit through the ties that were cutting into him and said: "Tomorrow I will bite Anangama's son, but I am going to tell you now about the medicine that can cure my bite. If you heal the child you will certainly be set free again."

16

So the snake carefully told him everything he needed to know, then tied him up again, slithered away and lay in wait behind Anangama's house.

When Anangama's little son came out at dawn the next morning, the snake bit him in his leg and the bite was so poisonous that everyone could see that the child would die that day. Anangama called out in despair: "Who can cure a snake bite like that?" And at just that moment a cockerel came along the path and said, "I think the huntsman you captured yesterday must know all about cures. Most huntsmen do."

So Anangama ordered the huntsman to be untied and to come to him. When the huntsman stood before him, Anangama asked, "Can you help my child?" and the huntsman replied: "Your son will recover even before today is out." He gave the boy the medicine and soon the child was better. Anangama thought about all of this and then he said: "You are a good man, for you have saved my child's life. I cannot believe that you wanted to steal my gold." And so the huntsman told him all that had happened and Anangama said: "I give you your life and your freedom, and the man who betrayed you will receive a just punishment." And so the wicked man was caught and punished for what he had done.

What big **ears** you have ... **!**

All the better to **hear** the hyena's unforgettable laugh!

Many Africans don't like hyenas because it is said that sometimes hyenas go to burial grounds and devour the corpses there. No wonder then that this animal has such a bad reputation and that people say hyenas are dirty, greedy and nasty. The Dinka and the Nuer from East Africa believe that humans no longer have eternal life because of the hyena. According to their legends, Heaven and Earth used to be connected by a rope. Old people used to climb up rope up to God so that He could make them young again before they climbed back down. But one day, wanting to put an end to this, a hyena cut through the rope and since that day, all human beings have to die. For the Kaguru in Tanzania, hyenas are in fact the witches of the animal world! The mask on the right here is from East Africa and has huge ears, attentive and upright. Hyenas feed on carrion, but they do also go hunting themselves. When they devour their prey they screech and snicker in such a strange way! You can see the teeth have been very carefully made, for hyenas have mighty jaws. They can crunch bones that would even be too much for a lion!

The hyena mask on this page is made by the Bamana in West Africa and is very different. It has long pointed ears and with its open mouth it looks as though it is just about to attack, although we can't see its teeth. But even without teeth showing this mask still seems eerie, perhaps partly because it is so dark. While the round-eared, East African mask goes right over the dancer's head, this West African mask is tied in front of the dancer's face. Young Bamana men, members of a secret society, wear the masks for specific occasions and the young boys who watch are supposed to learn that all good people never try to be inconsiderate, stupid or greedy.

Can sawfish really saw?

Some of the best boat-builders and seafarers in the world live on the Bissagos
Islands off the west coast of Africa. And of course sea creatures play an
important part in their lives: especially such dangerous looking ones as the
sawfish which can grow up to six metres long. It looks as though this triangular
mask represents a whole ray, but when you look more closely you can see that
it is only the fish's head. Its small eyes are very clear. Anyone who has
watched underwater-film of rays swimming will have seen how they
seem to glide weightlessly through the water as the tips of their fins
move gently up and down like the beating of a huge bird's
wings. The folded-over ends of the fins on the
mask look as though they are just starting to
move. But how is this mask worn? It
doesn't have any openings for
the dancer to look
through. In fact the dan-
cer wears it flat on his head
like a hat, with the saw pointing
forwards. To stop it falling off during the dance, it is
fastened with ties. This mask is unusual because it does not hide the
dancer's face. In its search for little fish and other creatures, a sawfish will stir
up the sea-bed with its saw. During the mask ceremony, which often lasts
for hours, the dancer copies these abrupt, violent movements of the sawfish.
And, while he is doing this, every so often he leans forwards so that the onlookers — like us here — can see the sawfish from above.

What a **mighty** mask!

It's a buffalo mask and gives a good impression of the solid power of these animals. Who would ever imagine that these ponderous animals can make themselves practically invisible in broad daylight? They hide in a thicket or in a waterhole and, although they are there, they are not easy to spot. A huntsman might easily think the buffalo is in front of him while all the time it is behind him and maybe getting ready to attack him! Buffalo can become absolutely furious — above all, when they have been wounded. People fear them. So the Tabwa and other peoples in Southern Zaire use the buffalo mask as a symbol of the power of their leaders.

The photograph shows that the artist has carved a mask that looks very like a real buffalo. Its heavy horns are curved and dangerously pointed. If this mask attacks during a dance the onlookers have to watch out for themselves. The artist has also not forgotten the buffalo's soft little ears. Its mouth is slightly open, its nostrils are slanted and its eyes are made of cowry shells.

Foto: Marc Felix, 1973

It's never a good idea

to make a buffalo angry !

And what is **that** supposed to be **?**

It is almost as big as a pig, has skinny legs and has long ears like a hare. It has a short neck, a rounded back, a long snout and an even longer tongue. And in order to eat up ants — because this is an aardvark — it can stick its tongue out as far as 30 centimetres! They are hardly ever seen during the day because they hunt at night. If it is being followed, an aardvark can bury itself in the ground in moments. The Tabwa say that when an aardvark suddenly finds itself in sunlight it just quickly puts its head underground leaving its behind sticking up in the air, but that is probably just a shaggy dog story because aardvarks would never be that stupid. The Tabwa are just having a little joke!

Aardvarks are seen as determined and careful and occur frequently in the art of many different African peoples. It is always easy to recognise an aardvark mask by its long ears and longish snout. Plant fibres are tied through holes on the wooden section of the mask and then woven into a hood. (This is how most African masks are made, only usually the fibres or pieces of material just hang downwards, as you will already have seen in some of the photographs.) The mask dancer puts the hood on over his head and can see out through the front directly under the aardvark's mouth. Although the mask is only painted in black and white, it is extremely effective and the artist has made the bast hood light and dark to match.

Foto: Marc Felix

left-tusked

To be

or

right-tusked,

... that is the question!

Did you know that elephants are left-tusked or right-tusked like people are left-handed or right-handed? In fact an elephant uses its tusks — like we use our hands — for all sorts of things: to dig for water, salt and roots, to get at trees and branches, as a weapon and to protect its trunk. The longest tusks that have ever been measured were 3.20 metres long and the heaviest weighed over 100 kilos! But the trunk is much more important. With it the elephant can grasp, lift, smell and touch, suck up water, make noises and do all sorts of other things besides.

Because of its size, strength and intelligence, the Bamileke in the Cameroon see the elephant as a symbol of royal power and also of wealth (because its ivory tusks are so precious). Elephant masks are worn by dancers at important occasions like the funerals of kings and queens and at harvest festival. The dance is carried out by the princes of the kingdom, who are all members of powerful secret societies.

The elephant masks you see here both come from the Cameroon grasslands and show how different the same animal can look depending on who the artist was. The wood on the fine, smooth mask was blackened using a piece of red-hot iron. It has elegant tusks and its trunk, stretched out forwards, is somehow much too long for the size of its head. One tusk seems to be more worn than the other .... On the other hand the mask on the right looks rather scruffy and has a lot of holes in it. A large piece has broken off the left ear and the wood is scratched and splintered — all signs of weathering, because in Africa the heat, the humidity and the termites all ruin things made of wood; and this mask is extremely old — already over 100 years!